Survivors, Saints and Sinners

Poems by

Sharon Waller Knutson

Cover art by Mary C. McCarthy
ISBN: 978-81-8253-913-6

First Edition: 2022
Rs. 200/-

Cyberwit.net
HIG 45 Kaushambi Kunj, Kalindipuram
Allahabad - 211011 (U.P.) India
http://www.cyberwit.net
Tel: +(91) 9415091004
E-mail: info@cyberwit.net

Printed at Vcore Connect LLP.

In memory of Ralph, Alfred, Phyllis and Benjamin Knutson

Acknowledgements

I thank the following journals for publishing these poems in one form or another:

Black Coffee Review: "*We need to reposition her in bed*,"

Muddy River Review: "Teton Valley Flood June 5, 1976."

One Art: "Sonnet"

Red Eft Review: "Free Falling," "Joe, Shoshauna and Sharon," "Silence is Golden," "Traipsing the Trailer to the Thrift Stores" and "Waiting for the Uber at the Assisted Living Facility."

Spillwords: "Night Noises."

Trouvaille Review: "September Storm" and "Winter Full Moon."

Verse-Virtual: "Inga, Phyllis and Joyce," "Motorcycle Grandma," "The Hospice Guy Kworker who delivers Hospice equipment nocks on the Screen Door," "The Last Supper," and "*There's a mouse in the house*."

Your Daily Poem: "Idaho Falls, Idaho - 1995" and "Rainbow Day."

Contents

Back Story

Teton Valley Flood June 5, 1976

1-Steamroller

He is about to put a new starter
in the black 1969 Oldsmobile,
when the sheriff shouts,
The Teton Dam busted
and the river is running
your way. It's time to evacuate
your mobile home park.

We flee to the hill
near Ricks College
where we watch
the wall of water
turn into a steamroller,
stripping the land from Sugar
City to Rexburg, tossing
like toys, the Texaco Station,
Trailer Park, Clyde's
Café, houses and vehicles
and drowning livestock.

We find our doublewide
five blocks away, logs
from the lumberyard
sticking out of windows,
and the Oldsmobile
molded by the river's
hands into one gigantic
round metal sculpture.

2- Missing Mare

Our four stallions –an Arabian,
Palomino and two Appaloosas -
stomp and stamp hooves
in their temporary stables
at the rodeo grounds,

missing our mare,
the sorrel quarter horse
with the white socks
and feet hobbled like a geisha
to keep her from running away.

Last we saw her, she was paddling
in the pasture trying to keep her
head above water, says a neighbor.
I don't see how she could survive.
The land is underwater now.

We drive up the road
expecting to find her carcass
when we look up and spot
the mare mud up to her chin
running towards us fast
and free without any shackles.

3-Surviving with Squatters

We buy a house and a barn
with the insurance money
and find a dark haired
man and red headed woman

about our age and a boy
and a girl about the same age
as ours sitting at the kitchen
table eating soup and bread.

The pastor said the house
was vacant and we lost
our house in the flood,
the man says. Maybe
it's because our baby
bumps are the same size
or we feel like family
that we let them stay.

We four sleep in one bedroom
and they four sleep in the other
until they get enough money
to buy a plot of land from us
and move in a double wide
and two families
displaced by the flood
sprout new water wings
and learn to swim again.

Survivors, Saints and Sinners

Remembering his daughter who lived
sixteen hours and the sorrow
that follows in the Great Depression,
he blesses his infant great granddaughter
by drizzling drops of Holy Water
on her head as his hands shake
from Parkinson's and several strokes.
To keep from falling, he grips
the handle of the walker, recalling
smelling of rot gut whiskey
and tossing the bottle as his teen
self leaps on the boxcar barreling
down the tracks, his feet catching
n the rail sending his shoes
scattering in the brush. Barefoot
he rides the freight train
from North Dakota to Montana
where he sleeps in a cemetery
and hops another boxcar to Idaho
where he gets a job picking
peas. Mormon missionaries
cleanse his body of alcohol
and tobacco with a bath
in the Teton River
to free him up to follow
in the footsteps of the saints
who were once sinners like him.

Right out of a Historical Romance Novel

Who's the tall dark haired guy?
asks the shy girl entering her cow
in the 4H Project at the county fair.
He's your neighbor's ranch hand,
her mother says. *Too old for you.*
He's pretty cute, she giggles.
He doesn't even glance her way.

Have you seen my cows? she asks
now sixteen straddling her sorrel
when she and the ranch hand
meet on the trail. *I heard a bell*
out back, he says and keeps
on striding. She finds a horse
wearing a bell but no cows.

Would you like to go to the movies?
he calls at the community college.
I'm going to be a nurse, she says.
I'm drafted and heading to war, he says
as they share popcorn in the theatre
and a kiss and hug in the parking lot.

Can you get Valentine's Day off?
I'll be in Salt Lake on furlough,
he asks from a pay phone. *Why?*

She asks. *I thought we'd get married.*
Her heart flops like her hair. *I'll ask.*
But nursing students aren't allowed
to marry until we graduate.

Okay, since you're marrying a soldier
and we're at war and you will be
a cadet when you graduate,
her supervisor says. *The weekend*
is yours but you have to work
on Valentine's Day. She grits
her teeth as she whistles.

Sweethearts for All Eternity

Home from leave during World
War II the soldier in uniform,
and the nursing student draped
in silk, satin and organza
pledge love for all eternity
on Feb. 16, 1945.

For sixty-eight years, she stands
by his side as they raise children,
chickens, cows and sheep
and as he studies to be a teacher
after a pine breaks his back,

and nurses him back to health
after a stroke steals his speech
and ability to swallow. She tries
to keep him alive as his chest
rattles like the cupboard dishes

during an earthquake, he chokes
and coughs like a chugging locomotive
and wheezes as his lungs leak
air like a punctured tire. But
he disappears as daylight dawns
two months before his 96th birthday.

Each year she thinks she will join
him, but eight years pass before
her legs swell and stiffen

like the frozen creek, she struggles
to breathe and her heart
flutters like a butterfly.

Her voice vacillating in volume
from a squeak to a whisper,
she greets guests at her 98th
birthday party from her recliner
and five days later, like Snow
White she falls into a slumber
knowing her prince is waiting
on the other side to awaken her.

Her Journal Tells All

June 28, 2011
I find him sitting on the doorstep
with skinned nose, forehead and elbow.
Says he fell on the sidewalk
and crawled to the patio.
He makes it into the house.
I bandage his nose.

June 30, 2011
He has cancer removed
on his forehead.
Looks like sunburn.
Doctor sends us home.

July 20, 2011
More skin cancer removed
this time from his forearm.
Looks like a burn. Wonders
if it will scar as we go home.

July 31, 2011
His feet are swollen
and he can't get his shoes on.
Emergency room doctors
take blood, x-rays and an EKG.
Say he's healthy as a 50-year-old
although he is 93.

Aug. 30, 2011
He trips on rocks while fishing
at Blackfoot reservoir and falls
hitting his head, leg and elbow.
Home from the emergency room,
he is getting up to go to bed
and falls backwards into the chair,
it tips over, barely missing hitting
his head on the stereo.

Sept. 3, 2011
We just finish dinner
and he tries to say
something and can't.
He talks fine when we get
to the emergency room.
Doctor diagnoses mini stroke.

July 31, 2012
We just sit down to dinner
and he says he is really dizzy.
When I ask him if he is okay,
he opens his mouth but no
words come out. I call 911.
They give him a cat scan.
No hemorrhaging. MRI
shows brainstem stroke.
Not expected to survive
because he can't swallow,
doctors say but he never
listens to doctors.

Aug. 31, 2012
At 3 am he falls out of bed
and takes me with him.
I get up but can't lift him
so he stays on the floor.
I call Hospice. Holly helps
get him up and orders
a hospital bed. Says his fever
is high and his oxygen is low.

Aug. 31, 2013
He isn't breathing very good
and I give him some morphine.
He is close to the edge of the bed
and keeps dropping his hand.
I am working on his obituary
when I hear a gasp
and he is gone at 9:10 am.
Wish he would have made
it to Oct. 26, his 96th birthday.

Like Mother, Like Daughter

June 5, 2011
I'm sorry, your brother is dead,
says the voice on the phone.
She remembers him playing
hide and seek with his nieces
and nephews at the family
reunion the year before as they
had as kids. *He is only 59,*
she says. *Pancreatic cancer*
is fast, the voice says.
He can't be dead. He's less
than two years older than me.

March 15, 2012
I'm sorry, your husband is gone,
the voice says on the phone.
She takes a big bite of the German
Chocolate Cake she baked
for his birthday 13 days ago.
When he left for Safeway's
this morning he said he'd
be home tonight. She swallows
the cake. *His heart stopped,*
the voice says. *He is only 59.*
We married three decades ago.
We have daughters and grandkids,
she says. *You have a wrong number.*

August 30, 2013
Your father is dying. Please come,
my husband tells his sister on the phone.
But Mom says he just has the flu.
Mom is in denial, he says.
Two days later he calls. *Dad is dead.*
She flies in and helps her mother
dress her father and supervises
his haircut by the mortician.
He looks just like he's sleeping, she says.

April 17, 2021
Hospice is here, my husband says.
One day mother is attending
a birthday party and the next
she can't walk or dress herself.
She asks to speak to her mother.
Did you wear a mask? What did
you eat? Is there mold in your walls?
Her brother says: *The nurse is here.*
Your mother may not live to be 98.
On her mother's birthday she calls,
How are you feeling? she asks.
Pretty good, her mother says.

Idaho Falls Idaho 1995

The ink barely dry on his divorce papers,
the farmer turned real estate broker
walks in the bookstore and tells me
he reads a book a day and wants to swap.
Then asks me for supper at a small café
across the river where we enjoy lobster
and baked potatoes and conversation
as smooth as the caffeine we sip until
we see the closed sign in the window
and the waitresses napping in their chairs.
Silver anniversary? the waitress asks
as he pays the check. *First date*, he says.
I nod and she laughs. *Such jokers.*

Like teenagers, we are eating corn
on the cob and shish kabob
in the bleachers at the Blackfoot Fair
as Tim McGraw sings, *I like it, I love it*
I want some more of it and we drive
in his white Buick to the top of the hill
above the tiny toy city on the tracks.
You kids go home to your folks, says
the policeman with the shiny flashlight.
I go home to my mother with melanoma
and he to his seventeen-year-old son.

Twenty-seven years later, mother long
gone, son with kids and wife of his own,
we eat grilled chicken and green beans

in Applebee's sitting smack dab in the spot
where the comfortable café once cuddled
the riverbank, but we skip the freeway
ride to the fair and pick up a DVD
by Sheryl Crow and relax in the recliner
in front of the DVD player and listen
to her sing, *Every Day is a Winding Road*
and pretend we are seeing her in person
as we revel in the landmarks of our life.

Caregiving

Caregiver Blues

In the pasture out back
of my mother-in-law's
Idaho home, a new calf
missing his mama
bawls and bellows

and the dozen other calves
join the chorus. Vanna spins
the wheel and contestants
buy a vowel and the washing
machine spins shirts and sheets.

Lawrence Welk and Myron
Floren play *Blue Heaven*
on their accordions
while the sky lightens
to eggshell blue.

Back home in Arizona,
a close friend dies
of breast cancer
and her ashes are spread
out in the desert. In town,

lightning strikes a palm tree,
and it burns like a giant candle
and the power shuts off
in our home where food
waits in the freezer for our return.

Night Noises

The sky turns into Fourth of July
fireworks as the sunset explodes
crimson, tangerine and magenta
and stars fall in the blackness.

The old water heater bubbles
and bangs like a canoe
sloshing in wavy water
and hitting the dock.

I think I must be back home
because I hear the big black bull
snorting and stomping but it is only
my husband snoring beside me.

I am sure the old washer is playing
percussion, but the sound is coming
from my brother-in-law's bedroom
as he breathes through clogged nostrils.

The doorbell rings and I run
In the living room to answer it
expecting a policeman or gunman
at this late hour. Fingering

the ringer from her hospital bed,
my 98-year-old mother-in-law
says her swollen feet and ankles
feel like she is walking in flames.

Feet thud and the floor creaks
in the double wide as the brothers
plod down the hallway narrow
as a mineshaft carrying flashlights.

The oldest turns her over, sits
her up and helps her stand,
and the youngest wheels her
to the kitchen where I give

her fentanyl. Once the fire
is extinguished we go back
to sleep until the sun splashes
us awake, the doorbell rings again,

baby robins chirp like crickets
in their weeping willow nest,
sausage sizzles on the stove
and a new day begins again.

Joe, Shoshauna and Sharon

Arizona must be hot,
Joe says as he stands
under a California redwood
scratching his scruffy beard.

Shoshauna is waiting
in Wisconsin, I say
as he opens the door
of his trashed truck,

crammed with carpenter
and car fixing tools.
Just in case, he says.
as we head for the highway.

On the 1-80 East passing
through Wyoming we spot
a buxom blonde in skinny
jeans staring at a tire flatter

than roadkill on a Toyota
on the side of the road
and hear a baby crying
from the back seat

piled with blankets, shirts,
boxes and baby clothes.
Joe pulls over, grabs
his lug wrench and jack

and removes the spare
tire from her trunk
as she hands me the blue
eyed baby and a bottle.

She peers down the road
like she's looking for the man
who left the rainbow
rimming her right eye.

Joe tosses the flat in the trunk,
hands her a fistful of greenbacks.
I'll pay you back I promise,
she says as she takes the baby.

Shoshauna shows up
in sunglasses in her sedan
at a rest top in Nebraska
and pulls out her picnic basket.

Joe grins under his floppy hat,
Shoshauna smiles, her dark
hair and my blonde hair
blanketing our backs as we chew

chicken and buttermilk biscuits.
Are your poems true stories? I ask.
I have to admit sometimes
I embellish, says Shoshauna.

Mine are true until the poem
finds its own truth, Joe says,
What about yours? But before
I can answer I wake up.in Idaho

and the bell is ringing
and the clock says 4:30 am
and we race to the hospital
bed to get my mother-in-law up.

Ben And His Grandmother

She holds him right after
he is born and sees the face
of an angel staring
up at her with blue eyes.
She watches him shearing
sheep with his grandfather
in his youth, fixes him breakfast
and washes his sheets
when he leaves home at sixteen
and attends the ceremony
when he gets his GED
and an associate degree.
She cheers him on when he
follows in his grandfather's
footsteps and joins the Navy
and sails off in a submarine.
She stands by his side
when he returns to bury
his other grandmother.
She looks forward
to his phone calls
every Christmas, Mother's
Day and her birthday
until the dark day
he dies at the age of forty-four
just six weeks before her.

Ain't it Just Grand?

My cell phone rings.
Is my grandma at your house?
my great grandson asks.
Not anymore. She just left,
I say before his mother,
my granddaughter chimes in.
He'd be shocked to know
he had three grandmothers
in the same house. Five years
old and a kindergartener,
he sets me straight to Sunday.
My grandma lives near me
and you're HER grandma.
Later when he sees
his great great grandma
snoozing in her recliner,
he asks: *Who's that?*
And after they are gone
and I call our daughter,
he answers her phone
and says: *It's Grandma.*
No great or great greats
just grand like a piano.
And that's just great with me.

Bionic Woman

She squats in her living room,
pretending she is batting a ball
with her newly unwrapped
stainless steel shoulder
so by the time she turns eighty
she'll be back on the tennis court.

I *know I'll never win another*
one of those, she says, gesturing
towards the shelf, where shiny
trophies line up like shoppers
at the Black Friday Sales.

Or beat my husband again,
as at eighty-three he wins
against young champions.
But I may best my daughter,
just nineteen years her junior,
if she lets me. She laughs.

Thanks to titanium knees
and hips, including a hip
she busted falling
on the court after colliding,
with another player
she is busy as a badger
babysitting great grandbabies.

It's hard to remember us
seventeen in the sixties
in bobby sox and loafers
our circle skirts ballooning
as we lay on our backs
on the table in study hall
belting out Elvis's *Hound Dog*
and scrambling to our feet
as the principal marches in
and growls, *My office, Girls.*

You want to take a shower?
she says, when I tell her my
joints are welded and I can't
get in or out of the tub
at my mother-in-law's house.
As she blow dries my hair
she says, *Remember how*
as teens we wanted to live
forever. I'm rethinking that.

Rainbow Day

In a purple plum dress,
flowing to her feet,
and white whipped
cream swirled hair
topped by a pink tiara
fit for a queen,

my mother-in-law
blows out two candles
commemorating 98 years
on a chocolate frosted
orange juice cake,
and in tangerine crop pants,

I serve strawberry parfait,
slices of turkey, ham
and cheese, cherry tomatoes
and garden leafy lettuce
to coiffured church ladies
and grand, great and great great

and we eat on brown tables
on the green grass under
the weeping birch and pine
as blue birds serenade
and the breeze cools our skin
in the scalding lemon sun.

Inga, Phyllis and Joyce

Like a dandelion gone to seed
blown in by the breeze, Inga arrives
early and alone, slips in and out.
But her name is on the mind of all
who attend the 98th birthday party
for Phyllis. *You're almost as old as Inga.*

Inga is the healthiest of us all,
says Joyce, who lost her hair
and a breast to cancer
and her husband to dementia
before her 90th birthday
just last spring, *Inga drove*
cross country alone to visit
grandkids in her nineties.

Phyllis rattles off everything
she's lost in the past years,
appendix, ovary and fallopian
tube, two giant gallstones,
gallbladder, parathyroid,
two cataracts and a husband,
as she stretches swollen
and heavy log like legs
in her living room hospital bed.

Inga has outlived two husbands
and she's still driving
and playing the guitar at jams.

Joyce laughs as she eats her chocolate cake
Two days later, Phyllis sends her son
with a birthday card to Inga's house
just a ways down the road. Huge hearts
decorate the posts and trees in Inga's yard.
Since her car is gone, she's at the church,
says Phyllis, *celebrating her 101th birthday.*

The Guest Who Doesn't Sign the Book

The scent of pine and birch
rides on a breeze through
the open screen door
and mingles with floral fragrances.

Helium balloons float above
the living room hospital bed
where my ninety-eight-year-
old mother-in-law sleeps.

Her ankles swell like the Snake
River after a summer storm
following the ebb and flow
of friends and family.

A shrill strangling sound summons
us from our bedroom down the
hall to glimpse a short stout woman
standing by the bed trilling

like the birds in the trees outside.
I know I am late but you know
I'd never miss your birthday party.
She smooths her wrinkled skin.

She disappears and we realize
she resembles the woman
in the oval frame with plaited
and piled cotton white hair.

As my mother-in-law awakens,
gravel crunches in the driveway
and a small car pulls onto the highway
and is swallowed by cumulus clouds.

Sonnet

She says her mother named
her Sonnet because she loved
Edna St. Vincent Millay and read
her *Love is Not Blind* in the crib.

In her Mickey Mouse voice,
she tells us she has rescued
a newborn wren that needs
to be fed every 30 minutes.

Left it in a cage in her two-bedroom
apartment along with the bulldog,
Border Collie, two Siamese
and five four-week-old kittens.

*Baby birds are fragile. Hope it survives
while I'm at work for three hours,*
she says grinning as Shirley Temple
curls fall on her forehead.

Cool, she says as I tell her again
to please hang up my mother-
in-law's silk blouses and slacks
and brand new birthday dress

and not wad them up and throw
them in the hamper like wrappers
and to wring out the wet towels
and hang them up to dry.

We are watching videos
when my mother-in-law
rings the bell rigged to her recliner.
As we rush in, she says, *Wake her up*!

Sonnet is sleeping soundly
and surprised when we shake
her shoulders and like a Stepford
Wife, she stands up and smiles

as she gently lifts my mother-
in-law from the recliner
and wheels her to the hospital
bed and tucks her in.

Carlos and the Cattle

In a silver Toyota, he shows
up saying he wants to rent
her pasture for the calves
his rancher boss gives him
as partial pay as a ranch hand.

No cows. They step on and break
the pipes, she says when she sees
the red Ram 2500 drive up the dirt
road. On her walker, she watches
at the window as seven chubby
calves peek through the tall
green grass. She melts
like the popsicle she sucks on.

She watches the calves calmly
eat hay from his steady hands
and cavort with his pre-school
children as they grow into cows
and not once do any hooves
crush the irrigation pipes
that pour water into the trough
and soak the pasture.

Sometimes she awakens
in the night to the sprinklers
hitting the double wide
and realizes it is midnight
and Carlos has finished

his shift and is watering
her lawn and the cows
and goes back to sleep.

Although they never meet
in person she asks if Carlos
and his family want apples
or strawberries from her garden
and he asks if her back
is still bothering her.
Carlos and the cattle
are still here after she is gone.

After

We need to reposition her in bed

the hospice nurse says as my mute
mother-in-[law lies in the hospital
bed on her back still as the statue
of liberty, parched lips pinched.
Slick as a magician, the nurse
slides her over to her other side
on a second silk sheet,
until she is facing the wall,
her stiff and staunch back to us.
The morphine should help her
sleep, she says as she fills
vials of the liquid painkiller
and instructs us to administer
the medicine every two hours.
Don't wake her if she is sleeping.
So we don't. We do peak around
and see one hand gripping the rail
and the other arm in the air
as she rests on an elbow.
She doesn't move a muscle,
but still we watch and wait,
not wanting to disturb her.
Finally at bedtime, my husband
shakes her shoulders
and she is a snow sculpture
with blue lips and eyelids
closed like Confucius
praying for peace.

The Hospice Guy Knocks on the Screen Door

This is my thousandth hospital bed
I've picked up and my last. The sun
shines on Siamese emerald green eyes
and carrot orange hair and beard.
I'm off to medical school, he says
dismantling the rails and sides
with his burly body and biceps.

What is your specialty? we ask
as he hands the blue egg crate
mattress to my husband.
Trauma. Emergency room. Blood
and guts. I want to be the doctor
no one wants to see. My husband
carries the mattress to the bedroom
for the grandkids to sleep on
when they come for the funeral.

Your wife passed? he asks
noting my husband's white hair.
as he lifts the frame over his head
like he is pressing iron. *My mother,*
my husband says, *She died*
in her sleep after her 98th birthday.
My husband holds the screen door.
Holy cow! That's how I want to go
but not for sixty-eight years.

He picks up the portable potty
and the folded wheelchair.
Got a toddler and one on the way.
My daughter won't let me cradle
her anymore.so I'm ready to hold
Baby Number 2 in my arms.
He carries the equipment as a breeze
blows in through the open door.

My wife says she wants me to die
a week before her so she can be
a widow for only a short while.
My husband signs the paper.
I tell her she better talk to the man upstairs
because I don't think that's in his plan.
Waves as he walks away. *You folks*
have a trauma free life and I hope
I never see either of you again.

Motorcycle Grandma

I flew higher on the dilaudid drip
than when I was in the helicopter
and the private jet, says the blonde
with turquoise eyes as we watch
the Hospice nurse destroy morphine
and fentanyl after my mother-in-law's death.

As we eat roasted chicken
and vegetables, she recalls
the sky bleeding blood
three years ago as she hangs
onto her husband on the Victory
Cross County motorcycle
as they cross the border
from Alberta to Montana.

A truck pulling a trailer
makes a U turn right in front
of the motorcycle blocking it
like a barrier and they slam
into the rig. *We had a room*
booked in Kalispell. But we
didn't make it that far.

She takes a drink of Pepsi.
We were wearing helmets
but we hit so hard it knocked
him out and he has no
memory of the crash.

Like a brahma bull rider,
she busts her back and ribs,
but I remember everything.

The medic in the chopper asking her
if she is in pain and stabbing
her with the needle twice. Waking
up and screaming, *I don't have a bra.*
and the emergency room attendant
showing up with her bag full
of clothes she left on the back
of the motorcycle at the scene.

The surgeon saying my guts
are pushed into my chest
and my belly has a hole
in it and he needs to fix it.
Her sister shrieking,
He only has a one-star rating
on the internet. He isn't operating.
Her rich relative showing up
in a private jet and flying her
to University Hospital in Salt Lake.

That wasn't the only accident
they had on the ten-day trip.
We were just starting out in Bliss
when I heard a whole bunch
of Harleys behind us. Wild Hogs
hit us bam from behind.
The motorcycle mamas blamed us
and tried to sell us heroin but we
would have none of that nonsense.

She changes the subject abruptly.
Jasper National Park is spectacular.
The Colorado Rocky Mountains
are grand, but the Canadian Rockies
are rockier. She rubs her shoulder
and grimaces in pain. *I still hurt*
but I'm alive. You should try it.

Waiting for the Uber at the Assisted Living Facility

Those Ukrainians really know
how to satisfy a sweet tooth,
says the man with the gray beard.
The honey in the Koliva tasted
heavenly and the fruit filled
Koliva was to die for. Five stars for sure.

But the hostess's hair was a disaster.
She looked like Little Orphan Annie
at 100 years old, states a woman
with wrinkles deep as ditches
and hair blue as the cloudless sky.
The Shepherd's Pie at the shindig
for the shaggy Scottish gal was delish.

Who can forget the roast pork and cabbage
at the celebration for the bald guy
with the bushy eyebrows from Estonia,
she adds while the beard brags;
The ham glazed with orange juice
and brown sugar at the gala
for the burly Brit was the best.

How do we get an invitation
to these fancy dinner parties?
the white poodle frizz asks.
No invitation necessary, blue hair
replies as the uber pulls up.
Just read the obituaries. The foreigners
serve the best funeral food.

That's My Niece

Who's the Judy Garland
sing alike? guests wonder
at my father-in-law's
80th birthday party,
as the seven-year-old
in pig tails sings,
Somewhere over the rainbow
blue birds fly, why can't I?

Who's the Celine clone?
someone asks as the blue
eyed blonde hits the high
notes with her seventeen-
year-old soprano
voice as she belts,
I was blessed
because you loved me.
at her grandfather's
90th birthday ball.

Who's the opera singer?
a parishioner asks
as her thirty something
voice soars like a nightingale
in the chapel as she warbles,
beyond the sunset blissful
morning, eternal joy
to celebrate the life
of her 98-year-old grandmother.

At 11 am Friday

There's a knock on the door
and the short woman
in the red smock
and the gray hair
stands there as she has
at that time every Friday
for the past four months.

But this time she isn't
carrying her portable
bag with shampoo,
curling iron, dryer,
and box of rollers.

She isn't racing
to the recliner
to wheel my mother-
in-law to the sink
where she shampoos
her white hair
when she is unable
to visit the salon
as she has for two decades.

This time her hands
are as empty as the
recliner. She is there
to pick out mementos
her client and friend

wanted her to have
after she was gone.

She picks up the green
Afghan her friend
had knitted to put
on her legs on chilly
nights as she watched
TV, an angel figurine
and a book of hymns
they sang together
in church every Sunday.

Did you like the way
I styled her hair
for the viewing? she asks.
Yes, she would have been
very pleased and glad
we had an open casket,
I say as we hug goodbye.

The Last Supper

My ninety-eight-year-old
mother-in-law leaves behind
a hungry family and pantry
and fridge filled with food
in cans, bottles and boxes.
The day before the funeral,
we serve strawberry jam
on sour dough bread,
canned pears, raspberry, cherry
and orange Jello with fruit
cocktail, four cheese lasagna,
potato salad with flakes
whipped with milk, diced ham.
sweet pickles and relish,
brownies and watermelon
to thirty offspring: three sons,
their children and grandchildren.
This is such a Grandma meal,
says the daughter of her daughter,
absent because of a mini stroke.
We pour into Idaho Falls
from Salt Lake City, Seattle
Charleston, Cincinnati,
Phoenix and Pasadena
for one more family reunion
and as we toss a Frisbee
and kick a ball before posing
for family photos in the warm
July sunshine we realize
this is the last time
we will all eat her food, stay
in her house and play on her lawn.

Making New Memories

South Paw

Throw with your right hand,
our sons admonish their sister
when she throws the baseball
and strikes them out. She tries
and they laugh as she turns spastic.
So she sticks with her left hand
striking out batters
and hitting home runs.

You're ambidextrous,
the high school basketball
coach says when he observes
her switching hands
as she dribbles down
the court or steals
the ball from her opponent.
He coaches her in the art
of surprise and score.

Teach me how to do it,
her kids and grandkids
say as they watch her write,
bat, throw balls and bowl
with her left hand.
When they try to imitate
her, their left hand
freezes like a robot
whose batteries are dead.
She smiles and says:
Guess I have superpowers.

Son-In-Law

Solid handshake even at eighteen,
he looks her father in the eye
and asks for our daughter's hand
in marriage as if it were a remake
of Father of the Bride. No one
is laughing when the movie
turns dark and she elopes
with the bad boy and breaks his heart.

However, he is willing to wait
for her to realize she made a mistake
and so he gets his bachelor's degree
and a corporate job
and takes care of his Air Force
mother still suffering from PTSD
while our daughter has three kids.
and a marriage that ends in divorce.

They write letters, emails and phone
over the years and they finally recite
the vows they'd written almost two decades
ago in the backyard of her baby brother
and she moves a teenager, pre-teen
and a three-year-old into the new house
he bought with his mother in the suburbs
Twenty years rock and roll like a river.

The kids leave home and his mother dies
of Alzheimer's leaving them with five

cats, two turtles and a squawking parakeet.
Now in his fifties he poses for family photos
with their six dark eyed grandchildren
who call him Papa and don't know or care
if his blood is running through their veins
or if his skin and eyes are the same color as theirs.

Mega Mama

Despite a botched up back
from a car crash
and a broken ankle
from stepping in a hole
while rescuing eighteen
ducklings from coyotes,
she puts on her boots
and shorts and scales
the mountain for agates.

While breasts from chickens
she chases all over the acreage
she shares with our son
sizzle on the outdoor grill,
she flicks through photos
on her cell phone of babies:
a blue-eyed Siamese kitten
sniffing the camera lens

while his brothers, sisters
and mama sprawl
on her bedspread,
like expensive mink stoles.
Then she navigates
to Facebook where our pony
tailed grown grandsons flex
muscles and stick out tongues
and their older sister blows kisses
as she poses in pink hair.

Free Falling

As we read the date, *May 8, 2009*,
in his grandmother's journal,
the image sticks in our minds
of the long and lanky legs
of our six-foot two son flailing
through the wet Washington
air like the wings of a hapless
heron as he falls thirty feet
and lands with a thud
on the hard concrete pavement.

We can still hear his voice woozy
and wavy as he fights his way
through the anesthesia following
the surgery to repair shattered bones
in his hip and both wrists. *I rolled*
like they taught me in the military
parachute training or I'd be dead.

We can still see him crawling
on his hands and knees to lift
himself into the truck to drive
his son to school and then sitting
in a wheelchair on the sidelines
as his son hits a homerun
in Little League Baseball.

Do you remember the date
you fell from the roof? we ask

as he calls on his speaker phone
as his weakened wrists
at forty-six steer the rig
through the rush hour
and his hip full of hardware
hurts in the humidity. *Nope,*
he says, *but I can't complain*
since I lived to see my boy
turn twenty-two in May.

Silence Is Golden

Use your words,
our daughter-in-law
tells our toddler grandson.
Lips zippered into a smile,
his bird hands flutter
please and *thank you*
as his blue moon eyes
sparkle like the bubbles
he blows before dancing
like a dust devil. *Doesn't*
talk because he's deaf,
she says. I holler his name,
he whirls and I wave.
He races into my arms
and plants a sloppy kiss
on my cheek and I know
this kid is right as rain.

75th Birthday

Don't do anything, my husband says.
We'll bake him an ice cream cake,
announces our teenage grandson
when his grandfather leaves the room.
I work on Saturday but we
can do it Thursday, says our son.
We'll just tell him you're expecting
a phone call and he needs to sign
papers, I say. *Good plan,* he says.
What are you plotting? my husband
asks on Thursday when the phone rings
and I talk softly. Our son says
you have to sign papers at 4 pm.
When we walk in the door
of our son's home, the phone
rings and they sign papers.
You're psychic, our son whispers
to me as his wife roasts Brussels
Sprouts in garlic and olive oil,
fries chicken and boils corn.
You want to stay for dinner?
our son asks. *Sure*, his father says.
When we walk in the back yard,
a banner flies, the toddler waves
a card and the teen hands his grandfather
gloves and a wood working tool wrapped
in separate colored paper. *Sorry,*
the ice cream is too hard for candles,
says our son as he cuts into chocolate

cake frozen with vanilla ice cream.
I'm so glad you did this, my husband
says as the sun sets though the pines.

Celebrating at Chili's

On her 43rd birthday,
our daughter-in law
sits sandwiched between
her toddler and teenager,
husband on the side.

Her nursing uniform
in the car in case
the clinic calls,
she dines on shrimp tacos,
black beans and iced tea,

while our son enjoys
a turkey club sandwich
with no avocados
and we savor the salmon
and garlic mashed potatoes.

Our fifteen-year-old grandson
eats a hamburger with tomatoes,
pickles and pineapple
and drinks pink lemonade,
sharing his order of fries

with his two-year-old brother
who sips apple juice, saying,
No, No, No, to buttered noodles
and mandarin oranges
as the waitress flits like a fly.

Shouldering the Burden

My prescription is ready,
his maternal grandmother
says from her sick bed.
He drives her Cadillac
to the drug store. Notices
the steps and bathroom
floor in her cottage
are falling down and replaces
them and the faucet.

I could use some gas
and groceries, his paternal
grandmother says. He drives
her in the Buick to the station
and the store. *I've burned*
all the kindling, she says.
So he chops and hauls wood.

In the spring, he rototills
his grandmothers' gardens..
In the summer he mows
and landscapes their lawns.
In the fall he rakes their leaves
And in the winter, he shovels
snow on their sidewalks.
When it is time for them to go,
he carries their caskets.

On his 43rd birthday, he shrugs
his shoulders as he slices

the sirloin steak sizzling
on his plate at LongHorn
Steakhouse realizing it is time
for him to relax and enjoy
the rest of his life.

Oldest Grandson

His small hands push the lawnmower
and scoop snow with the shovel
until he has enough greens to pay
for a perm for his single mother.

His lips rhyme lines in the car
with his sisters and his grandfather
and me as we ride the freeways,
the rivers and the rollercoasters.

His feet climb the ladders to repair
roofs so he can jitterbug and cha cha
in the ballroom dance competitions
while his brain aces the tests.

His fingers search the Internet
for my poems and he recites
them to his great grandmother
who snoozes and says *don't stop*.

He blows bubbles with his five-
year-old daughter, videos her dancing
draped in scarves and jewelry
and smiles when she calls him *Daddy*.

Zoie and the Piano

In the hospital having
potassium pumped
into her heart,
our oldest granddaughter
misses the funeral
of her great grandmother.
She calls and requests
the out of tune no name
piano for her four kids

Dead ringers for Sonny
and Cher in their teens,
Zoie and Lonnie,
now in their thirties
look more like Johnny
and June as they pile
out of their silver Nissan
Rogue hitched up to a U Haul
with our four grandkids
carbon copies of their parents
who race to the piano and play
chopsticks until we adults
haul it out the door.

The sky is bruised and the wind
batters the tarp and bends branches.
Zoie reads the weather report.
Winds at 80 miles per hour
We suggest they stay

until the storm blows over.
She insists they have to get home,
but still she lingers her fingers tracing
the collectibles and antiques
her great grandmother left behind
as if she is memorizing them in brail.

After the family hugs us goodbye
and piles in the SUV, there is a knock
on the door and Zoie stands there
as she did as a child sheepishly saying.
I left my phone in here. Her grandfather
calls her cell. We hear it ringing
outside and see a chubby hand holding
it out the window. She clings to us
like moss on a rock and says,
I am afraid I'll never see you again.

Now the race is on

And here comes pride up the backstretch.
Heartaches are goin' to the inside,
the radio blares, The race is on
and it looks like heartache.
And the winner loses all.

I remember my nephew at eight-years-old
dark eyes peeled on the ponies
as they race along the track. He stands
on the bleachers cheering for the loser
lagging behind, the long shot he picked
to win and convinced me to bet on,
because the odds were against him.

His horse picks up speed like the announcer's
voice, passing all the ponies predicted
to win. *I told you so*, he says as I collect
the winnings and take out my $2
and put the rest in his college fund.
We repeat the same scenario all summer.

Even after he stays high sniffing,
snorting, smoking and chugalugging
and drops out of high school
to tour with a rock band, with zero odds
of success, I bet my money on him
and when the announcer calls
his name in the university auditorium,

and he accepts his Masters of Fine Arts
Degree summa cum laude, I can see
that little boy shouting, *We won.*
When he joins us in the bleachers,
I grab his arm and hold it up as we shout
in unison as we did that summer, *We won.*

Panic Button

It all starts just a month
before my sister's 77th
birthday with her toddler
grandson screaming in pain
and clutching his stomach
when her son drops him off
to run to the store for diapers
for her five-month-old
grandson she babysits
three days a week while
the toddler goes to daycare.

Next thing she knows
the toddler is in the emergency
room, pronounced infected
with the dreaded disease
that closes down his day care.
Babysitting duty is suspended,
her son says coughing the C
word into his cell as he wipes
the noses of the baby and toddler.

Her heart sinks like the sun
when she hears her eighty-two
year old husband hacking
and wheezing as his battle
scarred lungs and heart struggle.
I'm sure you've got it,
says the diminutive Asian

doctor swabbing his nose.
The oximeter pinches his finger.
Oxygen level is low.
Hospital is the place for you.
But he shakes his head
like the Lion King.

When the test comes back positive,
he gets a shot as potent as whiskey.
You're eligible too, the doctor informs
her. *I'm frisky as a feline,* she says.
Just to be safe, the doctor tells
her to wear gloves and a mask
and sentences her to fourteen days
in quarantine. She pushes the panic
button, not being able to stand
one more minute without feeling
the baby's breath on her neck,
the toddler's tiny hand in hers.

Preparing the Probate

The Snake, the Plumber and the Home-owner

I smell gas, I say as I slip into my night gown.
My husband checks all the burners.
The sewer is backing up into the sink.
He pours Drano down the drain.

I need a plumber, he murmurs into his cell
in the living room, while the kitchen sink
gurgles. *May I speak to the homeowner?*
a lady with a lilting voice asks.

My mother owned the home and she died,
my husband says. *Sorry, we can't send*
a plumber without the permission
of the homeowner. Insurance won't pay.

My husband wishes he could summon
his mother's spirit to speak but he can't
so he drives to Home Depot
and rents a snake, but it's too short.

Your father took care of my father's
cows when he was sick and dying
so anything you need, says the Swede
stout and sturdy as the machinery he operates.

Do you have a tractor, backhoe
or a Bobcat? My husband asks

after informing him of the problem.
No, nothing like that, the guy answers.

I rented a power drain cleaner
but it's too heavy for me to haul
up the roof on the ladder
so I wondered if you'd help.

We'll see when I get over there,
the guy says. My husband turns
to me. *We need you to stand*
on the bottom rung of the ladder

to balance it so we don't both fall
to our deaths. But when the black
pickup pulls into the driveway
and my husband and his helper
do their juggling dance on the white
asphalt in the burning sun, I am
in the air-conditioned back bedroom
listening to the crowd clap and cheer

as musicians and comedians perform
in the Dolby Theatre and Howie, Heidi,
Simon and Sophie bicker. I turn off Hulu
and like magic the sink is dry and silent.

After The Burial

When everyone is gone,
we flip the wall switch
and on the seventies stereo,
Garth Brooks sings,
I could have missed the\ pain,
but I would have missed the dance
on country music radio,
and on an rpm record
Glen Campbell croons,
If you go away
on this summer day.

Then as we pass the end
table to pull the blinds
while day turns to night,
and sprinklers water
the green pasture,
Big Mouth Billy Bass
flops his fish tail
and belts, stayin' alive
We're stayin' alive.
and we breathe
in the cool breeze
and boogie to bed.

On The Way to File Probate Papers

The sky is gray as the wings
of the mourning dove
as we pass the church
and watch men in suits
carrying a casket to the hearse.

We recognize the same mourners
who crowded the pews
and thc facc in thc obituary
of the man our age who shook
our hands and said, *Sorry for your loss.*

We stop at George's and Jesse's
and the heavy set dark haired
man in his fifties mounts the mower
tractor tire and just like his dad
refuses payment, says, *Catch you next time.*

The clerk with the smile and wavy hair
weighing down her shoulders
like our widowed daughter-in-law
stamps the papers and tells us
to seal them and mail them.

After we leave the post office
the sky is blooming a brilliant blue
and the sprinklers are watering
the green grass and a red breasted
robin is singing along with the radio.

Day of the Zoom Probate Hearing

I can't go, My hacker will follow me
into the courtroom, my husband's sister
says from a thousand miles away.
Don't go unless you oppose me being
personal rep, Sis. She laughs.
No one wants that job. Good luck.

You have reached the Courthouse.
Pay your fine now, the automated
voice repeats as he calls the number
for thirty minutes until he sees
a friendly female face.
Welcome. Do you oppose?
she asks baby brother. *Nope.*
I was told to come and I'm here.

I apologize. The judge is tied up
in trial. He'll sign the papers right
away. Baby brother leaves his car
in the parking lot two hundred
fifty miles away and goes back
to work. Older brother sheds
his white shirt and tie in the hot
double wide and drives two miles
to the courthouse when his cell rings.

How was the hearing? his middle
brother asks from his sickbed
one hundred and seventy-five

miles away. *I got the position,*
my husband says. *You can't come*
in without a mask, says the masked
woman at the newspaper office
so he pays for the ad on the sidewalk
and then walks into the cool breeze
with a stride in his step.

At the Estate Sale

Tall as the pines, dark hair
cupping under his chin,
our 15-year-old grandson
shows up in the cold
drizzle with his 14-year-old
girlfriend, a short, smaller
version of himself and heads

for the garage. As his grandfather
bargains with a bulky farmer
over the grinder, he jumps
on the tractor mower to show
an old-timer in overhauls
how smoothly it cuts the grass.

Meanwhile she texts her auctioneer
father photos of the century old
beds, dressers, end tables, lamps
and La-Z-Boy red as a rose recliner
and Maple kitchen table purchased
at Ray's Furniture Store in the sixties
to determine their worth.

The customers in slickers plunk down
dollar bills and haul off housewares
worth many times more and pass
up a cookie jar advertised on Ebay
for $150, collectibles my in-laws

purchased in their travels abroad
and cut glass bowls worth hundreds.

After they leave like looters,
she lies on the plush sofa with a wet
wash rag on her forehead
and he massages her temples
and serves her soup with chicken
broth and noodles. Later they laugh
as they spar and tussle on the carpet
like two lion cubs in the zoo.

September Storm

Like a woman mourning
her dead baby, the wind
whines, wails and waves
the branches of the birch
as she weeps and bends
begging for mercy. Stray
leaves fly like bats
against a drab sky.

The Ponderosa Pine
shrugs and sways
its shaggy arms
as thunder claps
its heavy hands.
Lightning fingers
flash and point
at the window.

I huddle in the office
wondering if she's up there
warning us we did
something wrong
when I see a piece
of blue sky peeking
behind the cottony
white curtain of clouds.

Suddenly the sun
smiles, all is quiet

and I reckon she
thinks we did something
right and we lift
the lamb roast
and the potatoes
and vegetables
out of the oven
and say our blessings.

There's a mouse in the house,

says my husband as he shuffles
the deck at the kitchen table
and a gray rodent sleek as a greyhound
races across the kitchen tile
and dives under the refrigerator.

I saw him nibbling on the granola
wrapper she left on the counter,
pipes up my mother-in-law
as he skates across the carpet
and dives under the couch.

I can't find one mouse trap
my husband says. *Of course not,*
I always kept a clean house,
she says as the mouse skates
up the hall on the linoleum.

My husband grabs a skillet
and races after him. Returns.
He escaped into a counter hole.
Don't get blood on my clean towels,
she says. I look up home remedies
to get rid of mice on my laptop.

Cocoa powder. Red Pepper flakes.
Left cabinet, top shelf, she says.
It's then I look at the door and see
the mouse scampering outside
and remember she's been gone for months.

Traipsing the Trailer to the Thrift Stores

Our past packed in boxes,
on a maudlin Monday morning
we snake up Seventeenth Street
to Deseret Industries. The gray
building and parking lot
are empty as a mausoleum.
The gate is locked tight.

Google Gal guides us on
Boulevard past the boarded
up buildings where we sip
fountain sodas in the sixties
on swiveling suede stools
while waiting for a prescription
at the corner drug store.

.

And the A & W Drive-in
on G street where we
drink root beer
in frosted glass mugs
from bare legged bunnies
who hop car to car.
The microphones and trays
still hang from the poles
unused for sixty years.

To the striped and steepled
Salvation Army church
where they still serve soup

to starving strangers.
Sorry, we aren't taking any
more donations except for food.
Come back in January, the Santa
Claus look-alike tells us.

We google Goodwill
and head on Holmes
where the store stands
next to the Dollar Tree.
We take anything but tires,
mattresses and bed frames,
says the cheerful worker
who hauls away seventy-
five years of our lives.

New Beginnings

Teton Valley 2021

The flooded farmland
is now a metropolis,
the trailer park turned
into a mini mall,
the house a McDonald's.

The slick streets where Sundance,
Sparky, Rascal and Targee
tied to the truck
slipped and slid at the sound
of the honking horn

is a paved highway lined
with Albertson's, Arby's
Harbor Freight and Walmart.
The road where we found Fancy
near railroad tracks twisted

like pretzels is a greenbelt.
The eighteen miles of road
where he rode Rascal home
when the Arabian balked and backed
out of the horse trailer is a freeway

where flashy cars, trucks and RVs
flow like the flood waters
busting through the Teton Dam.
The house where we rebuilt
our lives is still standing like us.

Winter Full Moon

Awake in my pajamas
nibbling on fruitcake,
I stand by the window
on this winter night,
and watch the black bear sky
devour the magnificent mango
moon one bite at a time
while the countryside
sleeps beneath a soft
marshmallow crème frosting.
When the sky's appetite is satisfied
it melts into mouthwatering
coconut crème chocolate
and then swirls into strawberry
parfait before the apricot marmalade
sun is spread on blueberry toast.

The Christmas Card

On Christmas Eve Day
my husband wades
through knee high snow
up the hill to the mailbox.
The white over sized envelope
sits on the top of the pile
of advertisements and bills
as if to say: *Read me first.*

He doesn't open it because
it is addressed to his mother
who's been gone five months
with the name of his father's
childhood friend on the return address.
She used to dance with him
to make his father jealous.
Both have been dead for decades.

Raised to respect his parent's privacy
and not read or open their mail,
he says: *It could be a communication*
between two ghosts who haven't
reunited in the hereafter. I go through
her file of obits and find a survivor
with the same name as the sender.

Long after arthritis crippled her hands,
and electronics took over snail mail,
my mother-in-law would sit for hours
and write letters to all her friends

and family and tuck them inside
Christmas cards and mail them
right after Thanksgiving Day.
She'd eagerly trudge through snow
to collect Christmas cards from her mailbox.

She would enjoy this card, I say
as I open the envelope.
Inside is a photo of a sixty something
balding man with a gray goatee,
a brunette woman and three
thirty something children smiling
and wishing her joy, peace and love.
The sun comes out and it stops snowing.

New Year's Eve Memories

We ring in 1996, our first
New Year's Eve, in Idaho.
Our breath fogs up the car
windows and we slip and slide
on slick streets and sidewalks
and dine on prime rib, mashed
potatoes and plum pudding
at the Sandpiper and then drive
to the Stardust where we foxtrot,
tango, mambo and rhumba.
He in a black suit and tie,
I in a plum purple gown
sweeping the floor.

Our first New Year's Eve
in Arizona in 2001, we dine
on lamb chops and moussaka
at the Olive Tree in Tucson
in shorts and tank tops
and then drive to Old Tucson
where actors shoot it out
in the streets as crowds cheer
and a Miss Kitty look-alike
serves us coke in the saloon
and we listen to Kenny
Chesney sing in the stadium
before he becomes famous.

In 2010, our twelve-year-old
granddaughter flies from Salt Lake
to Phoenix to accompany
us to the Queen Valley Rec Hall
where my husband in jeans, boots
and a black hat plays his guitar
and sings while she and I
in long fringed dresses
and curls swing and stomp
with cowboys to country
music and rattle our
noisemakers at midnight.

In 2021, we come full circle,
back in Idaho snowed in since
Christmas Eve. We find lobster
tail and green beans in the freezer,
potatoes in the pantry
and bake them and drizzle
them with butter from the fridge.
Play gin rummy and then go
to bed hours before partiers
shout Happy New Year.

White Out

From Christmas Eve
to New Year's Eve
the blizzard rages
like an angry animal
flinging the snow against
the garage and house
piling it up knee high
until the white powder
and pale sky become one,
keeping us captive inside.

On New Year's Day
we split our last log
and burn it in the stove
and eat our last slice
of bread as the temperatures
drop and the snow ceases.
The sky turns blue and sunny
as a figure in a dark snow suit
and cap appears in the yard.

Stiff as the icicles hanging
on the house, the woman stands
on a black ATV and zips
up and down our driveway
pushing the snow against
the trailer and the trees
plowing a path for us
to drive to the store
for gas and groceries.

I think back to the 1950s
as machines carved a road
and built snow walls
so we could walk two miles
to school, our faces chafing,
our fingers and toes frozen
in cheap boots and mittens
in the frigid Montana air.

Portrait in Black and White

In his white wool sweater
and black slacks, mittens
and boots, Mr. Magpie
marches to the roof
of the garage and flaps
his wings like a conductor
in an orchestra. The warm
wind whistles like a clarinet
as it tosses Mr. Magpie
face first against the facia.
Singing soprano, he summersaults
to the roof of the house
where he toots the trombone
as the chinook creates
an ice sculpture
in the shade of the pine.

All Gone

That's what our toddler
grandson says as he opens
cupboards, drawers and doors
in the empty double wide, his voice
echoing off the walls and linoleum.

I love you papa, he says resting
his head against my husband's
heart not realizing he may be
a tall teen like his brother
when we see him again.

Lake Powell filled to the brim
with blue water where we swam
and caught trout and bass
is dry and sprawled out
in the Utah desert
like a thirsty lizard.

The Colorado River raced
and bucked like a bronc
at the bottom of the Grand
Canyon while we watched
from giant rocks, but now
it slowly slithers like a snake.

My in-laws - now ghosts -
gaze through gauze
as the bulldozer demolishes

their barn and mobile home,
backhoes dig trenches
in the pasture and destroy
Pine, Birch and McIntosh
trees planted as seedlings
half a century ago.

Watching Ironwoods,
Palo Verdes and Mesquite
blossom and bloom,
a thousand miles away
we wonder when they signed
the deal with the developer
before their deaths if they ever
imagined their farm as a subdivision.

THE AUTHOR

Sharon Waller Knutson is a retired journalist who lives in a wildlife habitat in Arizona. She has published a full book collection, *What the Clairvoyant Doesn't Say (Kelsay Books) and six chap*books including "Dancing With a Scorpion (Moon Journal Press,) *My Grandmother Smokes Chesterfields (*Flutter Press) *and Trials & Tribulations of Sports Bob* (Kelsay Books.) Her work has also appeared in many online and print journals.

www.ingramcontent.com/pod-product-compliance
Lightning Source LLC
Chambersburg PA
CBHW062111160726
48282CB00026B/752